OTHER BOOKS BY DANIEL HANCE PAGE

THE FIRST AMERICANS AND THEIR ACHIEVEMENTS
LIFE IS A FISHING TRIP
BEAR TRAP MOUNTAIN
WHERE WILDERNESS LIVES
MANY WINTERS PAST
THE JOURNEY OF JEREMIAH HAWKEN
TOLD BY THE RAVENS
THE MAUI TRAVELER
WILDERNESS TRACE
ARROWMAKER
INDIAN DAWN
TRAIL OF THE RIVER
PELICAN MOON
LEGEND OF THE UINTAS

RILEY, THE DOG VISITOR

A True Story for People of All Ages

DANIEL HANCE PAGE

Copyright © 2016 Daniel Hance Page.

All rights reserved. No part of this book may be reproduced, stored, or transmitted by any means—whether auditory, graphic, mechanical, or electronic—without written permission of both publisher and author, except in the case of brief excerpts used in critical articles and reviews. Unauthorized reproduction of any part of this work is illegal and is punishable by law.

Photos by Daniel Hance Page

ISBN: 978-1-4834-6118-2 (sc)
ISBN: 978-1-4834-6117-5 (e)

Because of the dynamic nature of the Internet, any web addresses or links contained in this book may have changed since publication and may no longer be valid. The views expressed in this work are solely those of the author and do not necessarily reflect the views of the publisher, and the publisher hereby disclaims any responsibility for them.

Any people depicted in stock imagery provided by Thinkstock are models, and such images are being used for illustrative purposes only.
Certain stock imagery © Thinkstock.

Lulu Publishing Services rev. date: 11/10/2016

FOR

Riley's family who allowed him to be free to be himself and have an happy life

Often heard was a reminder
"You should write a book about that dog."

RILEY

This is a story about a part of a city—like any city—with a small area of trees similar to any forest with the only characteristic distinguishing this location from any other is in the recognition that here wildlife is welcome. Here the neighbors are in agreement with enjoying the natural environment. Their properties, or back yards, join together forming an enlarged, mainly forested area that attracts wildlife.

A fox walks along the top of a five-foot high, cedar hedge then sits down to watch the first rays of morning sunlight spread across the landscape. The fox enjoys food placed in a wooden box on top of the hedge. Crows also come for the same specialties. A deer has visited along with a coyote and ground hog. There are also many permanent residents such as raccoons, rabbits and skunks along with red, gray and black squirrels in addition to chipmunks.

FOX ON AN HEDGE

Birds are as varied as they are numerous including wild turkeys. They come to get seeds provided in feeders and fresh water in birdbaths. The only unwelcome visitors are the unnatural predators, domestic and feral cats that come to kill. Wildlife finds many places and most cities to be dark and forbidding, lit only by paths of light shining from welcoming places. When invited, wildlife appears. Dogs are always welcome.

I was working on trees in the small forest at the back of the house, during winter, when I saw a pup checking the action. The young dog, apparently a mutt with a lot of collie in him and of brown, black and white markings, had been attracted by the sounds of work and was watching intently, a sign of intelligence because he did not rush in carelessly where he might not have been welcome.

I spoke to him in greeting and the tail wagged in

reply. I called him over and one thing led to another until we were in a wrestling match. The pup won. He had me pinned down in the snow on my back and he was sitting on my chest, seeming to be thinking, well I've got this guy down now what am I going to do with him? Having clearly come to a conclusion, the pup got up and started walking forward. Snowy paws flopped across my face before he took off my hat and started running. He was so small his paws stepped on the hat while he ran and he kept tripping. Both dog and hat were easy to catch. This game of taking hats, and later gloves especially work gloves, continued throughout the dog's life and he never surrendered these trophies if there was any attempt to recover them. If he was not pursued, he quickly lost all interest in the gloves or hats and discarded them.

The pup lived two houses up the street. The house in between was owned by a gardener. I asked the gardener if he had seen the new pup.

"Yes, I have," he replied.

"Do you know his name?" I asked.

"I'm not sure," he replied. "But I think he's Irish."

Later, I learned that the pup was called Riley. He

lived with a family who, being kind and thoughtful people, allowed Riley as much freedom as he proved he could enjoy while not intruding anywhere on anyone, and thereby keeping the laws that have non-intrusion as their purpose but could be unnecessarily restrictive if applied when not required. Riley did not need a lot of rule enforcement or other training because, as one of his family members said, "He just seemed to know." Another time, she said, "Riley doesn't have a leash." Recognizing Riley's good qualities, family members were able to allow him to be free to be himself.

The neighbors in our immediate area are friends and understood and enjoyed Riley's ability to have earned freedom. He visited where he was welcome and stayed away from places he was not wanted or where danger lurked. I once heard a distant shout for Riley to get away from someone's property. I saw Riley leave and he never went back. He also stayed away from moving cars.

Riley only barked for communication. Sometimes the gate would be closed on the fenced area behind the house where he lived. When he couldn't leave because the gate was closed, he would call with a bark and I replied with a greeting to him. When the gate was open, he would go visiting.

Riley seemed to understand most words spoken to him. He also had many ways of communication. He barked rarely and only for a purpose. If we were down among the trees and he heard someone at the house, he would bark while walking toward the house, occasionally looking back to see if I was paying attention.

Most of his ways of communication were silent. In very cold weather, he would shake his ears to tell me they were cold, or hold up a paw to indicate his feet were cold. One time, when he was walking in the lead along the path through the trees, he stopped, sat down in front of me then held up his paw to say his feet were cold. After they had been warmed, the walk resumed.

If, on an hot day, he was thirsty, he would go to the outside tap and wait for a drink of cold water taken from my cupped hands. Most communication came through the awareness of knowing.

In the wilderness, wildlife reacts differently to people according to their intentions. An hunter in a forest will say special skill is needed in order to find something to shoot while a person without a gun will see much wildlife. All residents of a forest fear aggression and respond favorably to kindness. Consequently, when people walk in a forest, they are received the same way they treat the forest. As one of innumerable examples, Andy Russell, from western Canada, said in the first part of his life he was an hunter and in later years a photographer. He noticed, as others have, a marked contrast in the way wildlife responded to him when he entered the wilderness with different intentions, one hostile and the other friendly. Such awareness is understandable considering the divine link between each part of life.

Because Riley was not our dog, we tried to not bring him into the house. He also preferred to be outside. Sometimes in the early morning, he tried to get a short inside visit.

He liked to be clean. If his feet were muddy during an early visit, he was pleased to have them washed, one at a time, in a bucket of warm water.

Inside, he liked to lie on the living room rug while I had a cup of coffee and read the newspaper. When he was ready to leave, he would stand up, look at me then I would let him out.

During one of these events, I had a cup of coffee on the table and was reading the newspaper while Riley was lying on the rug. After a short rest, he stood up and looked at me as his signal that he was ready to go out. This particular day, I held the newspaper up farther so I could not see his look and thereby couldn't let him out. Suddenly the newspaper I was holding bent inward as Riley's head pushed up against it. I continued to keep it up so I couldn't see him. Next his head came under the newspaper and I readjusted it so I could not see him. Again his head pushed under the paper then thrashed from side to side until I was left with nothing more than two handfuls of torn paper and he was staring at me as if to say, "Can you see me now?" This of course led to a wrestling match in the living room before we went to the door and he walked outside to continue the rest of his busy day.

When we did not receive mail delivery, there would be left in the mailbox an explanatory notice stating,

"DOG WAS OUT". I didn't tell them that the dog was supposed to be out because he wasn't our dog.

The ancestors and thereby relatives of today's dogs are the wild dogs—the gray wolves, coyotes and foxes.

Riley, the Dog Visitor

GRAY WOLF

Daniel Hance Page

COYOTE

Riley, the Dog Visitor

FOX

The wild relatives have to constantly use and exercise their intelligence in order to survive. They fight only in self-defense or to obtain food. Today's dogs, in many cases, have not had to similarly maintain or keep up their intelligence through constant diligence because their safety and food are provided by people. When wolves have been pursued by dogs, the wolves have been known to deliberately cross and re-cross highways because dogs have not had to be in highest alertness to survive and are often not careful crossing roads.

Riley inherited many of his abilities, not from his modern relatives, the domestic dogs, but more directly from his more distant ancestors, the wolves, coyotes and foxes. Like the wild relatives, Riley was particularly intelligent and made his own decisions, not always relying on people.

He fought only in self-defense. He did not bother

smaller dogs; but once, when challenged by a dog of similar size, Riley, with snarling and bared teeth, forced the other dog to retreat.

Like the wild relatives, Riley would not carelessly risk injury. In the middle of one night, I was awakened by Riley's steady barking at my side door. Knowing that he only barked for a reason, and this time he was calling for help, I looked outside and saw Riley, next to the side door and being aggressively approached by a large, black Rottweiler. I rushed downstairs, opened the door and Riley shot into the kitchen and watched while I got a shovel and drove off the attacker. Although I have met friendly Rottweilers, this particular dog was growling, and aggressively hunting Riley. I couldn't take Riley home in those circumstances and didn't want to phone the family in the middle of the night; thereby, he enjoyed sleeping on the living room rug and we walked to his house in the morning to report the reason for his absence.

In another incident, I saw Riley lying on a sidewalk on the far side of an intersection where three roads met and a lot of cars were passing in all directions. He was completely stretched out on the sidewalk and refusing to get up when called repeatedly by a man from the family and one of his friends. I walked over to this intriguing situation where Riley had just stretched out and refused to cross this intersection because there were too many cars. We started walking farther along a sidewalk bordering one of the roads to move away from the traffic and Riley immediately responded, got up and walked with us. We waited until there were no cars moving in either direction then we all crossed the street.

During an excursion when Riley was traveling with the family to visit a farm, he refused to get out of the car because outside there were chickens strutting around and Riley had never before seen such large birds. Like his wild relatives, for self-preservation, he avoided unknown or possibly dangerous situations.

One day, I was attempting unsuccessfully to start a fire in the fireplace at the back in an open area. Riley was watching from one of his resting places in the trees where he could often be found. As the wet wood refused to ignite in other ways, I made a mistake a person commits only once and dripped some gasoline on the wood, thinking that the air currents would remove any combustible fumes. When I tossed a burning match toward the wood, there was a whooshing bang of fire. I realized my error and would not make the same mistake again although the wood started burning. Riley stood up, gave me a look of disgust and went home, ignoring my assurances that everything was all right.

Even around the most careful person or dog, dangers lurk and we don't escape from all of them. While out for a walk with some members of the family, Riley got separated and went missing. Search parties were sent out everywhere to look for him. He was located the next morning at the pound.

While doing some wood carving at the back, I saw Riley taking his usual walk along the trail among the trees. A short time later, I heard one bark. After an interval there was a second bark followed by a pause then a third. Realizing he wasn't barking at anything—he was calling for help—I went to investigate and found him stuck between two trees. He had tried to walk between two cedar trunks. They had slipped past his shoulders then closed in front of his hips, catching him like a fish in a gill net. To make the situation worse, he sat down then couldn't get up. All he could do was call for help. I pushed the two cedar trunks away from his sides. When he felt the trunks release their grip, he walked out of the trap.

Riley, the Dog Visitor

ON THE TRAIL

One day, Riley was walking along the top of an high bank of snow when some snow caved in under his feet and he toppled over the bank coming to a stop with his back at the bottom and his feet pointing upward. He tried to get up by bringing his body up over his feet and couldn't move. He just looked over at me for help. I pushed my arm between the bank and his legs before bringing his legs up, over then down under his body. He walked away from this predicament and was pleased to be rescued. He also apparently thought the skyward movement with his legs might have been excessive roughing and he charged me, ready for wrestling.

Occasionally during wrestling matches, minor incidents occurred. One time, a paw slammed against my face with such force I briefly saw darkness and a flash of light. When I opened my eyes again, I saw Riley watching with a suspicious look on his face as if maybe this delay might be some kind of a trick.

In another incident, my elbow came up and accidentally caught Riley under the jaw. He stopped, smacked his jaws together a few times to make sure everything was all right then he was ready to continue.

During the earliest time, there was a necessity for the Native Americans to include hunting along with the domestication of crops to acquire food. All the hunters from the Indian nations could not diminish the number of wild animals, birds and fish. The first hunters also hunted respectfully, knowing that an healthy environment was essential for their own prosperity.

When the Europeans arrived, they also found some necessity for hunting in order to acquire sufficient food along with farming. At first finding wildlife to be in great abundance, European hunters did not recognize that the supply was limited and consequently they had little or no concern for conservation and the need to protect the environment for the future.

People kept changing the environmental situation until in modern times people are now abundant while wildlife and wilderness are in short supply. Hunting wild food is also not necessary except in remote areas where wildlife exists in sufficient numbers and some hunting is important for supplying food. Generally however, food is now less expensive to obtain and more abundantly provided through growing crops and domestically raising animals, birds and fish. Such domestic animals, birds and fish would not exist if they were not raised for food; thereby harvesting them is natural. Except in some remote areas, hunting wildlife is no longer needed or natural because food is provided domestically and the numbers of wildlife have been greatly reduced. The remaining wild creatures are in short supply and have not been raised for food or furs. They have their own lives to live and they are part of the natural beauty of the environment that must be protected and not killed. Each part has a purpose and is interconnected with all the others. As one of unlimited examples, the buffalo in Yellowstone National Park were diseased and also overgrazing the land until gray wolves from Canada were re-introduced. They removed disease and stopped overgrazing, thereby returning an healthy herd of buffalo to the park. Among many other purposes, including the enjoyment of their own lives and being part of the beauty of life, wolves, coyotes and foxes remove disease from wildlife by using diseased creatures for food.

Dogs are often considered by people to be their best friends while many people, along with government policies, tragically treat the wild relatives, gray wolves, coyotes and foxes, with complete misunderstanding and cruelty. As David Suzuki explained, while being interviewed, we owe it to ourselves to take care of the environment for our own benefit; yet we too often think we can wreck the environment without causing any harm to ourselves.

The wildlife that remains today has been greatly diminished in numbers and is threatened in many ways including loss of habitat, use of poisons, people who hunt for sport and killings by domestic cats that many people consider to be their pets. The domestic cat has never lost the ability to hunt and kill even when they are well fed by people and don't require food. Cats kill anything they can catch such as squirrels, chipmunks, rabbits and particularly birds.

Dogs have to be taught to hunt. Even wild dogs—gray wolves, coyotes and foxes—are not born with the ability to hunt or kill for food. They have to be taught to hunt by their parents. A naturalist, Bill Mason, raised wolves in captivity in order to film them. He tried to release them back to the wild where they would have to hunt to survive. When taken out to an herd of caribou, the wolves watched the caribou and would not hunt them. These wolves had to be taken back to town.

In towns and cities with small areas of trees, there is wildlife such as squirrels, chipmunks and birds. The main predator who kills this wildlife, aside from hawks, is the domestic cat. I try to scare them away from the small forest at the back as much as possible although they always return. The only thing in the world that Riley showed any sign of disliking was the domestic cat. He was always friendly, kind and in a good mood except when he saw a cat. At such times, fur stood up along his back, his teeth bared, he growled then charged in a raging fury that would send any cat up a tree. As long as they stayed in the trees he did not bother them. He didn't want any cats on the ground. I did not try to deter him from this habit because he was saving the lives of many birds, chipmunks, rabbits and squirrels.

Riley particularly liked the gardener and the gardener had a white cat that didn't seem to do any hunting. On one occasion when Riley and I were walking along the trail among the trees, he was in the lead and ahead of us we both saw the gardener's white cat. For the very first time, Riley did not charge. He merely stopped and watched. After an interval of indecision, he turned and looked back at me for help as to what he should do. I thought that I couldn't tell him to chase the gardener's cat and yet I didn't want to say to stop chasing cats; so he would have to make this decision himself. I resumed walking. Riley growled harmlessly at the cat then continued following the trail and the cat moved out of view.

One of Riley's favorite sports was chasing squirrels. When he saw a squirrel, he would get so excited he would tremble slightly then go into a motionless trance before eventually charging at the best possible time.

When he was concentrating on watching a squirrel, he refused to let anything distract him. I would occasionally tickle him around the stomach area and he would ignore this annoyance as he would a pull on his ear or even a tug on his whiskers. However, after chasing the squirrel, he would charge back in a wrestling attack.

Riley, the Dog Visitor

SQUIRREL WATCHING

During one event, he trapped a squirrel in a small hole in a tree. There seemed to be a likelihood that in such a situation the squirrel might get injured. One of the ladies in the family where Riley lives is a doctor. She came to the rescue, carrying her medical kit, saying, "I usually don't do squirrels." After checking the patient, she proclaimed him or her to be healthy. The healthy patient climbed the tree and quickly moved out of view among foliage.

Another time, Riley caught a squirrel in the cucumber patch. He had both front paws pressed down on some cucumber leaves and under the leaves there was a squirrel. Riley held this position until he got tired. Then he moved his paws and watched the squirrel escape.

In addition to squirrels, Riley also chased chipmunks. Because of the small size of chipmunks, I was concerned that one might accidentally get injured but wasn't sure how to tell

Riley to differentiate between squirrels and chipmunks—as they are both squirrels—and to chase one but not the other. After Riley almost stepped on a chipmunk during a pursuit, my brother said, "Riley, don't chase chipmunks!" Amazingly, Riley never chased one again although he continued his sport with the black and gray squirrels.

Chipmunks quickly learned to not worry about Riley and, when he was resting, they would even walk across his paws. With such an occurrence, he would take harmless snaps at them to get them off. Not chasing them was one thing but having them walking on him was more than his wolf ancestry and dignity could tolerate.

When he left his house and came to my place for a visit, he had to cross the gardener's property. Riley was friends with the gardener and often visited him.

Sometimes, as Riley was on his way over to visit me among the trees, he would get called back because the family had other things for him to do. Riley learned that sometimes he would have to sneak over. During these occasions, he would rush past the gardener who told me that Riley would go by as if to say, you don't see me. This isn't really me.

Associated with the occasional need to sneak over for a visit, Riley also got the notion that he should keep the fact that he and I were friends a secret. When I went to visit the family where he lived, he acted entirely differently—like a complete stranger.

When I first met Riley as a pup, he started the game of taking hats and expecting a pursuit in order to have them returned. He also took work gloves. I preferred to wear an hat while working in pine trees in order to keep pitch out of my hair; however, I couldn't wear one because Riley would attack and wrestle until he got it. I couldn't wear work gloves either, because he would charge out from among the trees at any time and struggle until he got the gloves.

While trimming trees, I walked past another neighbor's house. As Riley walked beside me, he carried my hat. Holding its bill in his teeth, the hat hung down in front of him. Looking out her window, the lady said, "Dan, is that your hat?"

"Yes, it is," I replied.

"That's the cutest thing!" she exclaimed.

Riley, the Dog Visitor

COLLECTING TROPHIES

Games were always being played. While we were walking along the woods trail, Riley stopped to check a scent. I walked farther ahead until the trail curved sharply around a fish hut. I got down on the ground on the far side of the hut to ambush Riley as he followed the path. After waiting for what seemed to be an unreasonably long time, I sensed a presence beside me. I turned and found myself eye to eye with Riley. He had a smiling, humorous look on his face. I had tried to catch him and he had caught me.

During breaks, I sometimes slept in the fish hut on one of its long, side benches. If Riley visited during such occasions, he would also sleep or rest on a rug covering the floor. When a person, who had come to visit, was told that I was resting down in the fish hut, this person opened the hut's door and came face to face with a very large dog. Having no way of knowing the dog was friendly, the visitor retreated in shock, exclaiming, "Oh! I didn't know he was in there!" Riley continued moving forward then stepped outside and I shouted, "He's friendly."

When Riley visited, he liked to become part of anything that was happening. During one of his visits, my brother and I were bringing a load of firewood into the basement. From a pile beside the house, I handed wood through an open, basement window to my brother who then stacked each piece in a woodbin. In the basement, there were very few sticks that Riley would like to chew. However, outside, the ground was littered with sticks. If Riley selected chewing sticks from those carpeting the ground, he would not be sufficiently part of the work crew. Therefore, when chewing wood was needed, he stepped forward, entirely filled and blocked the loading window, pushed his head inside and waited to be given a chewing stick. He initially held in his jaws each selection he was given then, if he didn't think it was suitable, he'd drop it and wait for the next offering. This selection process continued until he received a chunk he liked. If he rejected up to approximately four sticks at a time, he would hear, "Riley that's a good one. Take that one."

He would then accept that stick and moved away from the window to stretch out and begin chewing while the wood loading process could continue.

After a short time, he would come back, block the window again, stopping the whole wood procedure, push his head through the window and wait to be given a new piece of chewing wood. All three workers were part of the wood operation and gradually, with chewing stick entertainment provided, the wood was moved into the house. At no other time, before or after the wood loading operation, was Riley ever observed showing any interest in chewing on a stick.

Riley got his meals and water at home. However during visits he, when the occasion was appropriate, got included with some treats.

When I grill steaks at the fireplace back among the trees, an extra steak is always added to the preparations. During one of these events, when I was grilling steaks for guests, Riley visited. A light rain started just before the steaks were ready so the people moved inside a protected shelter and the steaks, as they became cooked, were taken inside to the guests.

Riley did not like to get wet. He usually didn't visit during the rain, or, if it started while he was out, he would rush to a shelter or go home. This particular day, however, he sat out beside me in the rain and watched the steaks being grilled. He apparently thought that if I was grilling steaks, he would get one.

Sirens announced the arrival of a fire truck before a man and woman, in uniform from the fire department, arrived to say they had received a call from a person complaining about a fire. They were surprised to find a guy and a dog grilling steaks in the rain and jokingly declared the fire to be burning under very safe conditions. The only complaint they had was about getting the call.

The woman and man from the fire department left to get out of the rain and there remained Riley and I beside the fire, watching two last steaks on the grill. I put a fork in one, lifted it up then dipped it in a container of clean, cold water to change the meat from sizzling hot to moderately warm. Next I cut out the bone because cooked bones are brittle and will splinter, being harmful if swallowed. Lastly, I picked up this deliciously scented, warm steak and gave it to Riley. He slowly sank his teeth into the prize then turned away and walked toward nearby trees. I have served a lot of steaks but likely none have been more enjoyed than that one.

Riley did not wander. He visited only a few closest neighbors and was very popular with all of them. He also received the best possible care from his family.

One day when the family was going to be away for a short time, a neighbor was given the role of watching Riley then before this neighbor went to work, Riley was to be put in the family's house.

I heard about this particular assignment because the neighbor came over to tell me that Riley didn't want to go into the house and the neighbor couldn't catch him. The neighbor asked for help. I told him I would look after Riley until the family members returned. The neighbor said his instructions were to put the dog in the house so that was what had to be done.

We walked over to the house and Riley came with us. We opened the door and I mentioned for Riley to go inside. He went in then turned around and gave me a look of condemnation as if to say, how could you do this to me?

Riley liked to rest among the trees. Sometimes, when he was relaxing, I would crawl toward him on hands and knees. When he noticed this happening, he did not want to see it and at first always looked away. While turning away, he made a decision then either stood up and charged or stretched out and refused to be disturbed, ignoring anything that was done to get his attention. Even tickling along the stomach and between the pads on his feet or pulling ears and whiskers failed to get a reaction.

When Riley was in one of his resting times of not wanting to be disturbed, some people visited and with them they had a pup. The pup did everything to get Riley to play such as climbing over him, nipping paws and even poking the claw on a paw up Riley's nose; but Riley ignored everything and continued resting.

Each person is an island and unique in his or her own way while also being connected by the divine link to other people and all parts of life, enabling people and wildlife to understand each other. Although individually unique, they all have the spiritual connection in common.

The bond that occurs between a person and a dog, much as with other aspects of life, is a connection between kindred spirits such as occurs between people. Thereby a dog is often referred to as a member of the family. Dogs and people are individually unique, making the bonds always different.

Riley received wonderful care at home. When he got older and had health problems, he received every medical assistance and even had a doctor in the house he could call in the morning.

Riley added much company, entertainment and humor to the neighborhood. He represents the success that comes from kindness and consideration. He had these and more good qualities and when he also received them from others the results spread to become a light that could not be extinguished. If more people applied these qualities to each other as well as birds, animals, fish and other parts of the environment most obstacles would vanish into success beyond our wildest hopes and dreams.

Riley's abilities enabled him to be free to be himself, keeping the spirit of the law without needing its restrictions such as leash or constantly closed gate on a fence. Although the days of his visits came to an end, his presence continues by spirit, through memory and now in a story.

ABOUT THE AUTHOR

Daniel Hance Page is a freelance writer with nineteen books published and others being written. His books are authentic stories filled with action, adventure, history and travel including Native American traditions and spiritual insights to protect our environment in the smallest park or widest wilderness.

Manufactured by Amazon.ca
Bolton, ON